Illustrator
Howard Chaney

Editor
Stephanie Jona Buehler,
M.P.W., M.A.

Editorial Project Manager
Ina Massler Levin, M.A.

Editor in Chief
Sharon Coan, M.S. Ed.

Art Director
Elayne Roberts

Cover Artist
Larry Bauer

Product Manager
Phil Garcia

Imaging
Richard Yslava
James Edward Grace

Publishers
Rachelle Cracchiolo, M.S. Ed.
Mary Dupuy Smith, M.S. Ed.

GEOGRAPHY BRAIN TEASERS

CHALLENGING

Author

Jodie Weddle Proctor

Teacher Created Materials, Inc.
6421 Industry Way
Westminster, CA 92683
www.teachercreated.com

©1998 Teacher Created Materials, Inc.
Reprinted, 2000
Made in U.S.A.
ISBN-1-57690-213-7

TABLE OF CONTENTS

Introduction 3

Maps and Resources 4

The World

World Map 5

Analogies Around the World 6

Which One Does Not Belong? 9

World Geography Sandwiches 10

This Map Is Making Me Hungry! 11

Money, Money, Everywhere! 12

Matching Continents and Native Animals . . 13

Place Names of the World. 14

Mountains and Rivers of the World. 15

Seven Wonders of the Ancient World 16

The World in ABC Order 17

North America

Map of North America 18

North American Analogies 19

Which One Does Not Belong? 22

U.S.A. Geography Sandwiches 23

Mexico Geography Sandwiches 24

Web Sites of North America 25

Web Sites of the U.S.A 26

North America Direction Connection 27

Before & After Puzzles 28

States of the U.S.A. 29

North America in ABC Order 30

South America

Map of South America 31

South American Analogies 32

Which One Does Not Belong? 35

South America Geography Sandwiches 36

Web Sites of South America 37

South America Direction Connection 38

South America in ABC Order 39

Africa

Map of Africa 40

African Analogies 41

Which One Does Not Belong? 44

Africa Geography Sandwiches 45

Web Sites of Africa 46

Africa Direction Connection 47

Africa in ABC Order 48

Europe

Map of Europe 49

European Analogies 50

Which One Does Not Belong? 53

Europe Geography Sandwiches 54

Web Sites of Europe 55

Europe Direction Connection 56

Europe in ABC Order 57

Australia

Map of Australia 58

Australian Analogies 59

Which One Does Not Belong? 62

Australia Geography Sandwiches 63

Web Sites of Australia 64

Australia Direction Connection 65

Australia in ABC Order 66

Asia

Map of Asia 67

Asian Analogies 68

Which One Does Not Belong? 71

Asia Geography Sandwiches 72

Web Sites of Asia 73

Asia Direction Connection 74

Asia in ABC Order 75

Answer Key 76

INTRODUCTION

Geography Brain Teasers provides the opportunity for the instructor to teach critical thinking, research, and map reading skills in one lesson. Helpful resources to complete the brain teasers include encyclopedias, geographic dictionaries, and maps. The first section is entitled "The World"; thereafter, the book is divided into sections corresponding to the six inhabited continents of the world. Each section includes analogies based on geography, science, and history facts.

Here are ideas and tips for teaching students to make analogies:

1. The first step is to learn to read the analogy. An example of an analogy is as follows:

   Austin: Texas::_____:Florida

   The analogy is read, Austin is to Texas as *what* is to Florida?

2. Students who are beginners in solving analogy puzzles may find it helpful to ask a question about the first part of the analogy. For example, what is the relationship between Austin and Texas?

   Students can find the answer by looking at a map of Texas or using an encyclopedia to discover that Austin is the capital of Texas.

3. Students can then apply the relationship of the first two parts of the analogy to the second. In the example provided, the student should realize that he is now looking for the capital of Florida. Using a map or encyclopedia, the student will locate the capital of Florida and will complete the analogy as follows:

   Austin:Texas::<u>Tallahassee</u>:Florida

4. The student may check an analogy by reading it as two sentences. For example, Austin is the capital of Texas. Tallahassee is the capital of Florida. If the sentences are logical, the analogy is probably correct.

5. Additionally, on each page of analogies the student is asked to write an analogy. Students should be encouraged to express original ideas. In the beginning, students may be allowed to write an analogy based on one of the analogies already on the worksheet.

If the student gives an answer which differs from that in the answer key, give credit if the student can show logical reasoning for the answer.

The brainstorming pages are included to allow students to increase fluency. It is recommended that grades not be given on these pages. After a brainstorming session, allow students to share their ideas. If a student has recorded an original idea, he or she should place a star in the margin beside it. If other students thought of the same idea, it should be underlined. In this way a student can determine how much of his or her work is original and how much is similar to that of others in the class.

MAPS AND RESOURCES

Included in this book is an outline map of the world as well as clearly labeled maps of the six inhabited continents, including countries. The maps are not detailed enough for students to obtain all the answers needed to complete the activities but are included for your convenience if you are using the exercises in a setting where other resources are not available. In such a case, direct the students to complete as many answers as possible given the resources on hand. You may also direct students to fill in the maps to make them more complete for their own use.

If you are using the exercises in a full classroom setting, however, you should direct students to use whatever resources are necessary to find the answers. Atlases with colored maps, encyclopedia maps with overlays, globes, Internet Web sites, and social studies texts will all be helpful, as will access to books on the library shelves. A good adult dictionary with place names listed in its appendix may also prove useful.

You may be able to obtain free maps from local automobile clubs, consulate offices, and travel agencies. You may also wish to make some of the following technical resources available in your classroom.

Technology

Broderbund. *MacGlobe & PC Globe* and *MacUSA & PC USA*. Available from Learning Services, (800)877-9378. disk

Bureau of Electronic Publishing Inc. *World Fact Book*. Available from Educational Resources, (800)624-2926. CD-ROM

DeLorme Publishing. *Global Explorer*. Available from DeLorme Publishing, 1995. Fax (916) 482-4350; http://www.theexplorer.com. CD-ROM

Macmillan/McGraw-Hill. *World Atlas Action*. Available from Learning Services, (800)877-9378. disk

MECC. *The Amazon Trail, Canada Geograph II, The Oregon Trail, The Yukon Trail,* and *USA Geograph II*. Available from MECC, (800)685- MECC; in Canada, call (800)624-2926. CD-ROM and disk

Mindscape. *World Atlas*. Available from Educational Resources, (800)624-2926. disk

National Geographic. *Picture Atlas of the World*. Available from Educational Resources, (800)624-2926. disk

Newton Technology. *GEOvista Tutor*. Available from William K. Bradford, (800)521-2009. disk

Queue. *Atlas Explorer*. Available from Educational Resources, (800)624-2926. disk

Software Toolworks. *World Atlas*. Available from Learning Services, (800)877-9378. CD-ROM and disk

WORLD MAP

ANALOGIES AROUND THE WORLD – 1

Analogy puzzles are thinking games involving relationships between paired items. Stating the relationship between the given pair of the analogy will give you the key to solving the second pair. Use a world map and reference books to solve these analogies. Number 1 is done for you.

1. London:Great Britain::_____*Canberra*_____:Australia
   (Capital:country)(Think:London is to Great Britian as <u>what</u> is to Australia.)

2. Italy:Europe::Zaire:_____

3. Emu:Australia::rhea:_____

4. Mississippi delta:Gulf of Mexico::Nile delta:_____

5. Native Americans:North America::_____:Australia

6. Nebraska:Kansas:_____:South Australia

7. Mount McKinley:North America::_____:Australia

8. Aswan High Dam:_____::Hoover Dam:Colorado River

9. Horses:herd::lions:_____

10. Yangtze River:Asia::_____:North America

11. _____:U.S.A.::prime minister:Australia

12. Lake Superior:North America::Lake Victoria:_____

13. Mexico:North America::Thailand:_____

14. Bear:cub::kangaroo:_____

15. Lion:Africa::tiger:_____

Write your own analogy of the world:

_____:_____::_____:_____

ANALOGIES AROUND THE WORLD – 2

Analogy puzzles are thinking games involving relationships between paired items. Finding the relationship between the given pair of the analogy will give you the key to solving the second pair. Use a world map and reference books to solve these analogies.

1. New Delhi:India::_____:Canada

2. Brazil:South America::Pakistan:_____

3. Bison:North America::kangaroo:_____

4. Cape Horn:South America::Cape of Good Hope:_____

5. English:U.S.A.:_____:Netherlands

6. Europe:Africa::North America:_____

7. Mount Elbrus:Europe::_____:South America

8. Hawaii:Pacific Ocean::Madagascar:_____

9. Impala:lion::kangaroo:_____

10. Volga River:Europe::_____:Australia

11. Canada:U.S.A.::Switzerland:_____

12. Sahara Desert:Africa::Mojave Desert:_____

13. Bay of Biscay:_____::Hudson Bay:Canada

14. Anaconda:South America::cobra:_____

15. Canary Islands:Africa::Philippine Islands:_____

Write your own analogy of the world:

_____:_____::_____:_____

ANALOGIES AROUND THE WORLD – 3

Analogy puzzles are thinking games involving relationships between paired items. Finding the relationship between the given pair of the analogy will give you the key to solving the second pair. Use a world map and reference books to solve these analogies.

1. Cairo:Egypt::_____:Mexico

2. Canada:North America::Australia:_____

3. Koala:Australia::panda:_____

4. Guggenheim Museum:New York City::Louvre:_____

5. "The Star Spangled Banner":U.S.A.::_____:Australia

6. Suez Canal:Mediterranean Sea & Red Sea::

   Panama Canal:_____

7. Mount Everest:Asia::_____:Africa

8. Rocky Mountains:North America::Atlas Mountains:_____

9. Beaver:North America::platypus:_____

10. Nile River:Africa::Amazon River:_____

11. Rhode Island:Alaska::_____:Western Australia

12. Pyramids of Giza:_____::Mesa Verde:U.S.A.

13. Matterhorn:Alps::Mount Everest:_____

14. Mount St. Helens:U.S.A.::Mount Vesuvius:_____

15. Morocco:Africa::Chile:_____

Write your own analogy of the world:

_____:_____::_____:_____

WHICH ONE DOES NOT BELONG?

Listed below are four geographic areas of the world. In each set, three of them have something in common with each other, while the fourth does not. Circle the area that does not fit and then tell why.

1. Libya, Egypt, Zaire, Turkey

   Why? _____

2. Madagascar, Cuba, India, Japan

   Why? _____

3. Alaska, Canada, U.S.A., Mexico

   Why? _____

4. Pacific, Arctic, Mediterranean, Atlantic

   Why? _____

5. Algeria, Chad, Turkey, Spain

   Why? _____

6. Hawaiian, Canary, Marshall, Caroline

   Why? _____

7. South America, Africa, Australia, Antarctica

   Why? _____

8. Tasmania, New Zealand, Queensland, New South Wales

   Why? _____

9. Brazil, Zaire, South Africa, Ecuador

   Why? _____

10. Somalia, Angola, India, Australia

    Why? _____

Write your own "Which one does not belong?"

_____   _____   _____   _____

Which one does not belong? _____

Why? _____

WORLD GEOGRAPHY SANDWICHES

Sandwiches are made with two pieces of bread and a filling in the middle. In these geography sandwiches, you are given the "bread" but not the "filling." Study a globe or a map of the world to make a proper sandwich.

1. North America _____ Europe

2. Northern Hemisphere _____ Southern Hemisphere

3. Australia _____ New Zealand

4. Europe _____ Asia

5. Africa _____ Australia

6. North America _____ South America

7. Eastern Hemisphere _____ Western Hemisphere

8. Australia _____ Antarctica

9. Europe _____ Africa

10. Australia _____ South America

11. South America _____ Africa

12. Tropic of Cancer _____ Tropic of Capricorn

13. Africa _____ Asia

14. South America _____ Antarctica

15. Asia _____ North America

Make your own sandwich:

_____ _____ _____

10

THIS MAP IS MAKING ME HUNGRY!

Many foods are named for the place where they were first made. Other foods share their names with places in the world. Read the following clues to help find the location of these yummy place names.

1. It is a kind of mustard and a city of Europe.

    Where do you go to find Dijon? _____

2. It is a kind of sandwich and a city of Europe.

    Where do you go to find Hamburg? _____

3. It is a pepper sauce and a state in North America.

    Where do you go to find Tabasco? _____

4. It is a red wine and a city in Western Europe.

    Where do you go to find Bordeaux? _____

5. It is a cold cut and a city in Europe.

    Where do you go to find Bologna?_____

6. They are two kinds of cheese and two cities in Europe.

    Where do you go to find Gouda and Edam? _____

7. It is a kind of orange and cities in Europe and the U.S.A. are named for it.

    Where do you go to find Valencia? _____

8. An American might call it a hot dog, and it is a city in Europe.

    Where do you go to find Frankfurt? _____

9. It is a brand of chocolate and a city in the U.S.A.

    Where do you go to find Hershey? _____

10. It is a cheese and a village in Europe.

    Where do you go to find Cheddar? _____

11. It is a hot southwestern dish and a country.

    Where do you go to find Chile? _____

12. It is two slices of bread with ham, cheese, etc., in the middle and a borough in Europe.

    Where do you go to find Sandwich? _____

13. It is a citrus fruit and a city in Western Europe.

    Where do you go to find Orange? _____

14. It is usually part of the Thanksgiving feast and also a country.

    Where do you go to find Turkey?_____

15. It is a kind of steak and a plain in Europe.

    Where do you go to find Salisbury?_____

MONEY, MONEY, EVERYWHERE!

Each country of the world has its own basic unit of money. Match the countries listed below with the word used there for the basic unit of money.

Country		**Units of Money**
1. Mexico	_____	balboa
2. U.S.A.	_____	bolivar
3. South Africa	_____	dollar
4. Great Britain	_____	drachma
5. France	_____	franc
6. Germany	_____	guilder
7. Greece	_____	krona
8. India	_____	lira
9. Japan	_____	mark
10. Italy	_____	markka
11. Spain	_____	peseta
12. Israel	_____	peso
13. Austria	_____	pound
14. South Korea	_____	rand
15. Panama	_____	ruble
16. Venezuela	_____	rupee
17. Netherlands	_____	schilling
18. Russia	_____	shekel
19. Finland	_____	won
20. Sweden	_____	yen

12

MATCHING CONTINENTS AND NATIVE ANIMALS

The animals listed below are native to a specific continent. The word native means that the animal orginally lived in a certain place. For example, a hippopotamus is native to Africa because that is where it originated, even though hippos are found in zoos around the world. List each native animal with its corresponding continent.

anaconda	kangaroo	ostrich
Bengal tiger	Kodiak bear	panda
bison	koala	pine marten
camel	llama	Pyrenean ibex
cheetah	lion	rhea
cobra	nightingale	skunk
coyote	northern raccoon	sloth
elephant	Norway lemming	spectacled bear
fallow deer	numbat	Tasmanian devil
giraffe	orangutan	wombat

North America

_____

_____

_____

_____

_____

Europe

_____

_____

_____

_____

_____

Asia

_____

_____

_____

_____

_____

South America

_____

_____

_____

_____

Africa

_____

_____

_____

_____

Australia

_____

_____

_____

_____

PLACE NAMES OF THE WORLD

When people moved from place to place in the world, they often gave the new area where they settled names from the "old country." Listed below are cities and countries in Europe that were used as place names in the United States. Use an atlas, geographical dictionary or reference books to finish the chart. In some instances, the word "New" precedes the American place name.

European City, Country, or District	City in the United States	State
1. York, England		
2. Cambridge, England		
3. Lincoln, England		
4. Plymouth, England		
5. Salisbury, England		
6. Reading, England		
7. Bern, Switzerland		
8. Birmingham, England		
9. Rome, Italy		
10. Paris, France		
11. Saint Petersburg, Russia		
12. Manchester, England		
13. Athens, Greece		
14. Valencia, Spain		
15. Orleans, France		
16. Waterloo, France		
17. Memphis, Greece		
18. Odessa, Russia		
19. Cleveland, England		
20. Frankfurt, Germany*		

Spelling for American city is slightly different.

MOUNTAINS AND RIVERS OF THE WORLD

Using a globe, maps, and reference books, complete the charts below. For the chart on rivers, you will need to find the longest river on each continent, its length, and the location of its mouth (name of the body of water into which the river empties). For the chart on mountains, you will need to find the tallest mountain, its height, and the country in which it is located.

Continent	Longest River	Length	Mouth
Africa	_____	_____	_____
South America	_____	_____	_____
Asia	_____	_____	_____
North America	_____	_____	_____
Europe	_____	_____	_____
Australia	_____	_____	_____

Continent	Tallest Mountain	Height	Location
Asia	_____	_____	_____
South America	_____	_____	_____
North America	_____	_____	_____
Africa	_____	_____	_____
Europe	_____	_____	_____
Antarctica	_____	_____	_____
Australia	_____	_____	_____

SEVEN WONDERS OF THE ANCIENT WORLD

The structures listed below were built between the years 3000 B.C. and 476 A.D and were known collectively as "The Seven Wonders of the World." Use a reference book to complete the chart, listing the country and continent where each wonder was located, and the date each was built.

Structure	Country	Continent	Date
1. Colossus of Rhodes	_____	_____	_____
2. Hanging Gardens of Babylon	_____	_____	_____
3. Pyramids of Giza	_____	_____	_____
4. Statue of Zeus	_____	_____	_____
5. Mausoleum at Halicarnassus	_____	_____	_____
6. Lighthouse of Alexandria	_____	_____	_____
7. Temple of Artemis	_____	_____	_____

Now list the structures in the chronological order in which they were built.

1. _____

2. _____

3. _____

4. _____

5. _____

6. _____

7. _____

THE WORLD IN ABC ORDER

In the first column, list a country of the world for each letter of the alphabet. In the second column, write the name of the continent in which the country is located.

	Country	**Continent**
A		
B		
C		
D		
E		
F		
G		
H		
I		
J		
K		
L		
M		
N		
O		
P		
Q		
R		
S		
T		
U		
V		
W		
X		
Y		
Z		

MAP OF NORTH AMERICA

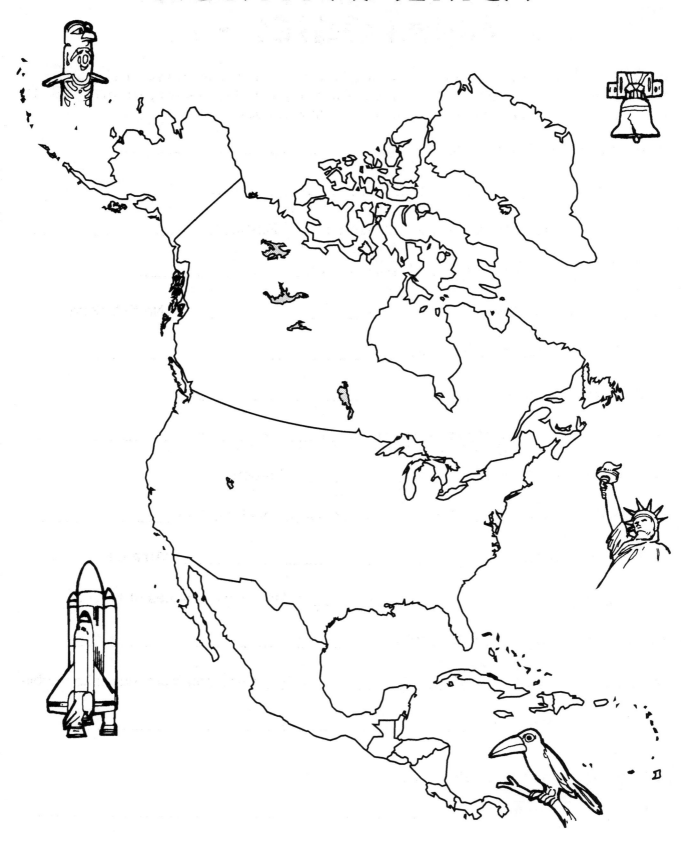

NORTH AMERICAN ANALOGIES – 1

Analogy puzzles are thinking games involving relationships between paired items. Finding the relationship between the given pair of the analogy will give you the key to solving the second pair. Use a map of North America and reference books to solve these analogies.

1. Utah:Colorado::Mississippi:_____

2. Hawaii:50::_____:1

3. Thomas Jefferson:William and Mary::George H. W. Bush:_____

4. Columbia River:Pacific Ocean::Mississippi River:_____

5. Harrisburg:Pennsylvania::_____:North Dakota

6. Chief Joseph:Nez Perce::Cochise:_____

7. Sonora:Mexico::Idaho:_____

8. Abraham Lincoln:16::Theodore Roosevelt:_____

9. Atlantic Ocean:Georgia::_____:Oregon

10. Yellowstone National Park:Wyoming::Grand Canyon National Park:_____

11. Red River:Texas::_____:Arkansas

12. Quebec:_____::Alaska:United States of America

13. Wisconsin:Badger State::New York:_____

14. Statue of Liberty:_____::Jefferson Memorial:white marble

15. Cherokee:U.S.A.::Aztec:_____

Write your own North American analogy:

_____:_____::_____:_____

NORTH AMERICAN ANALOGIES – 2

Analogy puzzles are thinking games involving relationships between paired items. Finding the relationship between the given pair of the analogy will give you the key to solving the second pair. Use a map of North America and reference books to solve these analogies.

1. Arkansas:1836::Ohio:_____

2. Franklin D. Roosevelt:twelve::John Quincy Adams:_____

3. President:Vice President::Governor:_____

4. Arizona:Mexico::Washington:_____

5. Illinois:Wisconsin::Iowa:_____

6. Jimmy Carter:Democrat::Zachary Taylor:_____

7. Carlsbad Caverns National Park:New Mexico::

   Mammoth Cave National Park:_____

8. Nevada:Carson City::Rhode Island:_____

9. Snake River:Idaho::Allegheny River:_____

10. New Hampshire:1788::Montana:_____

11. John Adams:Unitarian::Ulysses S. Grant:_____

12. U.S. President:four::U.S. Senator:_____

13. George Washington:1732::John F. Kennedy:_____

14. white pine:Michigan::_____:California

15. Sacramento:California::_____:Ohio

Write your own North American analogy:

_____:_____::_____:_____

NORTH AMERICAN ANALOGIES – 3

Analogy puzzles are thinking games involving relationships between paired items. Finding the relationship between the given pair of the analogy will give you the key to solving the second pair. Use a map of North America and reference books to solve these analogies.

1. Geronimo:Chiricahua::Sitting Bull:_____

2. Oregon:Beaver State::South Carolina:_____

3. Bill Clinton:Hillary::Harry S Truman:_____

4. Florida:Georgia::_____:Colorado

5. Quanah:Nokoni (Nocona)::Pocahontas:_____

6. Dwight D. Eisenhower:Denison, TX::Grover Cleveland:_____

7. Montpelier:Vermont::_____:Kansas

8. Tepee:Comanche::hogan:_____

9. Abraham Lincoln:_____::John F. Kennedy:Lyndon B. Johnson

10. Connecticut:white oak::West Virginia:_____

11. Show Me State:Missouri::Sooner State:_____

12. Nashville:Tennessee::_____:Nebraska

13. Lake Ontario:New York::_____:Ohio

14. Mexico City:Mexico::_____:Canada

15. Pilgrims:_____::Christopher Columbus:Santa Maria

Write your own North American analogy:

_____:_____::_____:_____

WHICH ONE DOES NOT BELONG?

Listed below are groups of four items in categories such as rivers, lakes, etc. Three items in the group have something in common; the fourth item does not belong. Circle the item that does not belong and then tell why.

1. Mississippi, Missouri, Red, Mexico

   Why? _____

2. California, Washington, Kansas, Oregon

   Why? _____

3. Utah, Indiana, Wisconsin, Ohio

   Why? _____

4. Atlanta, Houston, Denver, Sacramento

   Why? _____

5. Saskatchewan, Ontario, Alaska, Alberta

   Why? _____

6. Iowa, New Mexico, Tennessee, Louisiana

   Why? _____

7. Florida, Maine, California, North Dakota

   Why? _____

8. Superior, Michigan, Huron, Erie

   Why? _____

9. Idaho, Nevada, Kentucky, Arizona

   Why? _____

10. North Carolina, Arizona, Montana, New York

    Why? _____

Write your own "Which one does not belong?"

_____   _____   _____   _____

Which one does not belong? _____

Why? _____

U.S.A. GEOGRAPHY SANDWICHES

Sandwiches are made with two pieces of bread and a filling in the middle. In these geography sandwiches, you are given the "bread" but not the "filling." Study a map of the United States to make a proper sandwich.

1. Mississippi   _____   Georgia

2. North Dakota   _____   Nebraska

3. Wisconsin   _____   Michigan

4. New York   _____   Rhode Island

5. Oklahoma   _____   Texas

6. California   _____   Utah

7. Texas   _____   Mexico

8. Illinois   _____   Ohio

9. Arizona   _____   Texas

10. Missouri   _____   Illinois

11. Canada   _____   Mexico

12. Vermont   _____   Maine

13. Minnesota   _____   Missouri

14. Pacific Ocean   _____   Nevada

15. Washington   _____   California

Make your own sandwich:

_____ _____ _____

MEXICO GEOGRAPHY SANDWICHES

Sandwiches are made with two pieces of bread and a filling in the middle. In these geography sandwiches, you are given the "bread," but not the "filling." Study a map of Mexico to make a proper sandwich.

1. Guerrero _____ Chiapas

2. Baja California _____ Sonora

3. Chihuahua _____ Nuevo Leon

4. U.S.A. _____ Central America

5. Durango _____ San Luis Potosi

6. Yucatan _____ Tamaulipas

7. Sinaloa _____ Jalisco

8. Coahuila _____ Texas

9. Tabasco _____ Quintana Roo

10. Guanajuato _____ Hidalgo

11. Isla Maria Madre _____ Isla Maria Cleofas

12. Sonoro _____ Nayarit

13. Chihuahua _____ Zacatecas

14. Vera Cruz _____ Guerrero

15. Jalisco _____ Queretaro

Make your own sandwich:

_____ _____ _____

WEB SITES OF NORTH AMERICA

The three largest countries in North America are Canada, the United States and Mexico. Each of these countries has several states. A Web site has been created for each state, using its capital city as the address. Decode the following addresses to find the state and country. (Note: These are not actual sites!)

	State/Province	**Country**
1. www.winnipeg.geo	_____	_____
2. www.carson.city.geo	_____	_____
3. www.albany.geo	_____	_____
4. www.baton rouge.geo	_____	_____
5. www.helena.geo	_____	_____
6. www.raleigh.geo	_____	_____
7. www.edmonton.geo	_____	_____
8. www.juneau.geo	_____	_____
9. www.austin.geo	_____	_____
10. www.hermosillo.geo	_____	_____
11. www.salem.geo	_____	_____
12. www.toronto.geo	_____	_____
13. www.santafe.geo	_____	_____
14. www.durango.geo	_____	_____
15. www.augusta.geo	_____	_____
16. www.monterrey.geo	_____	_____
17. www.victoria.geo	_____	_____
18. www.sacramento.geo	_____	_____
19. www.concord.geo	_____	_____
20. www.ciudadvictoria.geo	_____	_____

Write your own North American Web site addresses:

_____   _____

WEB SITES OF THE U.S.A.

If each state of the U.S.A. had a Web site on the Internet, what might its address be? Some states might want to use the name of a national park located within its boundaries as an address. Read the following addresses and find out the state that might list it as an address. (Note: These are not actual sites!)

1. www.grandcanyon.geo _____

2. www.grandteton.geo _____

3. www.bigbend.geo _____

4. www.rockymountain.geo _____

5. www.mammothcave.geo _____

6. www.craterlake.geo _____

7. www.everglades.geo _____

8. www.glacierbay.geo _____

9. www.yosemite.geo _____

10. www.hotsprings.geo _____

11. www.haleakala.geo _____

12. www.mountrainier.geo _____

13. www.windcave.geo _____

14. www.shenandoah.geo _____

15. www.carlsbadcaverns.geo _____

Write your own Web site addresses for a state in the U.S.A.:

_____   _____

NORTH AMERICA DIRECTION CONNECTION

Look at a map of the United States. Given the location of a particular state and a direction in which to go, determine the state that is your final destination.

1. From Kansas go west to _____.

2. From Arkansas go north to _____.

3. From Georgia go south to _____.

4. From North Dakota go east to _____.

5. From Colorado go west to _____.

6. From Wyoming go north to _____.

7. From Vermont go south to _____.

8. From Mississippi go east to _____.

9. From North Carolina go west to_____.

10. From Indiana go north to _____.

11. From South Dakota go south to_____.

12. From Connecticut go east to _____.

13. From Nevada go west to _____.

14. From Alabama go north to_____.

15. From Oklahoma go south to _____.

16. From Florida go north to _____.

17. From New Mexico go west to _____.

18. From Kansas go north to _____.

19. From Delaware go west to_____.

20. From Vermont go east to _____.

BEFORE AND AFTER PUZZLES

Many of the men who have served as president of the U.S.A. share the name of a city, while others have had cities named for them as an honor. In these puzzles, a president is named first, followed by a state which has a city with the same name. Use a map or encyclopedia to find the city name which correctly completes the puzzle.

1. James _____ Louisiana

2. Thomas _____ *City* _____ Missouri

3. Abraham _____ Nebraska

4. Grover _____ Ohio

5. William H. _____ Michigan

6. Lyndon B. _____ *City* _____ Texas

7. John Quincy _____ Massachusetts

8. Ulysses S. _____ Nebraska

9. Zachary _____ Michigan

10. Bill _____ Arkansas

11. George _____ District of Columbia

12. Martin _____ Arkansas

13. John _____ Texas

14. James _____ Wisconsin

15. Andrew _____ Mississippi

16. Richard _____ Texas

17. James K. _____ Pennsylvania

18. Calvin _____ Arizona

19. Theodore or Franklin D. _____ New York

20. Harry S. _____ Arkansas

28

STATES OF THE U.S.A.

Use a reference book to locate the nickname and capital of each of the states listed below.

State	Nickname	Capital
1. Illinois		
2. Utah		
3. West Virginia		
4. Texas		
5. Michigan		
6. Delaware		
7. Kentucky		
8. Alaska		
9. Vermont		
10. Rhode Island		
11. North Dakota		
12. New York		
13. Georgia		
14. Tennessee		
15. Wisconsin		
16. Kansas		
17. Indiana		
18. Connecticut		
19. Washington		
20. California		
21. New Mexico		
22. Minnesota		
23. Pennsylvania		
24. Mississippi		
25. Wyoming		

NORTH AMERICA
IN ABC ORDER

Picture yourself on the continent of North America. Look around. What do you see? Think of at least one sight you might see for each letter of the alphabet and list your ideas below. (Hint: Think of the different land areas, man-made structures, animals and people.)

A _____

B _____

C _____

D _____

E _____

F _____

G _____

H _____

I _____

J _____

K _____

L _____

M _____

N _____

O _____

P _____

Q _____

R _____

S _____

T _____

U _____

V _____

W _____

X _____

Y _____

Z _____

MAP OF
SOUTH AMERICA

SOUTH AMERICAN ANALOGIES – 1

Analogy puzzles are thinking games involving relationships between paired items. Finding the relationship between the given pair of the analogy will give you the key to solving the second pair. Use a map of South America and reference books to solve these analogies.

1. Buenos Aires:Argentina::_____:Colombia

2. Peru:Pacific Ocean::Guyana:_____

3. Guyana:Brazil::Paraguay:_____

4. Paraguay River:Paraguay & Brazil::Amazon River:_____

5. Rhea:bird::guanaco:_____

6. Angel Falls:Churun River::Iguacu Falls:_____

7. Chile:Spanish::Suriname:_____

8. Quito:Ecuador::_____:Trinidad and Tobago

9. Argentina:Republica Argentina::Ecuador:_____

10. Suriname:Guyana::Argentina:_____

11. Guyana:Guyana dollar::Chile:_____

12. Cayenne:French Guiana::Lapaz and Sucre:_____

13. Chinchilla:rodent::vicuna:_____

14. Paraguana Peninsula:_____::La Guajira Peninsula:Colombia

15. Toucan:bird::manatee:_____

Write your own South American analogy:

_____:_____::_____:_____

SOUTH AMERICAN ANALOGIES - 2

Analogy puzzles are thinking games involving relationships between paired items. Finding the relationship between the given pair of the analogy will give you the key to solving the second pair. Use a map of South America and reference books to solve these analogies.

1. Brasila:Brazil::_____:Suriname

2. Gulf of Corcovado:Chile::San Jorge Gulf:_____

3. Venezuela:Colombia::Argentina:_____

4. llama:mammal:black caiman:_____

5. Salado River:Argentina::Maranon River:_____

6. Ecuador:Pacific Ocean::Uruguay:_____

7. Argentina:Spanish::Brazil:_____

8. Asuncion:Paraguay::_____:Guyana

9. Venezuela:Republica de Venezuela::Uruguay:_____

10. Trinidad and Tobago:Venezuela::Falkland Islands:_____

11. Bolivia:peso boliviano::Surinarne:_____

12. Tropic of Capricorn:Chile::_____:Ecuador

13. Piranha:_____::sloth:herbivore

14. San Francisco River:_____::Colorado River:Argentina

15. Giant anteater:ants and termites::nutria:_____

Write your own South American analogy:

_____:_____::_____:_____

SOUTH AMERICAN ANALOGIES – 3

Analogy puzzles are thinking games involving relationships between paired items. Finding the relationship between the given pair of the analogy will give you the key to solving the second pair. Use a map of South America and reference books to solve these analogies.

1. Santiago:Chile::_____:Peru

2. Falkland Islands:Atlantic Ocean::Galapagos Islands:_____

3. Uruguay:Argentina::Peru:_____

4. Magdelena River:Colombia::Xingu River:_____

5. bushmaster:reptile::tapir:_____

6. El Misti Mountain:Peru::Aconcagua:_____

7. Ecuador:Spanish::Guyana:_____

8. Montevideo:Uruguay::Caracas:_____

9. Bolivia:Republica de Bolivia::Peru:_____

10. Lake Poopo:_____:Lake Maracaibo:Venezuela

11. Argentina:peso::Ecuador:_____

12. Chile::Pacific Ocean::Brazil:_____

13. Coati:mammal::ibis:_____

14. Corcovado Gulf:Chile::Gulf of Guayaquil:_____

15. Marmoset:tropical rain forests::Galapagos tortoise:_____

Write your own South American analogy:

_____:_____::_____:_____

WHICH ONE DOES NOT BELONG?

Listed below are groups of four items in categories such as rivers, lakes, etc. Three items in the group have something in common; the fourth item does not belong. Circle the item that does not belong and then tell why.

1. Brazil, Costa Rica, Argentina, Chile

   Why? _____

2. Rio Negro, Madeira River, Tapajos River, Tocantins River

   Why? _____

3. Bolivia, Brazil, Colombia, Ecuador

   Why? _____

4. vicuna, guanaco, rhea, alpaca

   Why? _____

5. Suriname, Ecuador, Brazil, Uruguay

   Why? _____

6. Lima, Caracas, Santiago, Rio de Janeiro

   Why? _____

7. llama, anaconda, ostrich, spectacled bear

   Why? _____

8. Maracaibo, Amazon, Madeira, Parana

   Why? _____

9. Trinidad, Tobago, Falkland, Ecuador

   Why? _____

10. Paraguay, Peru, Venezuela, Argentina

    Why? _____

Write your own "Which one does not belong?"

_____   _____   _____   _____

Which one does not belong? _____

Why? _____

SOUTH AMERICA GEOGRAPHY SANDWICHES

Sandwiches are made with two pieces of bread and a filling in the middle. In these geography sandwiches, you are given the "bread" but not the "filling." Study a globe or a map of the world to make a proper sandwich.

1. Chile   _____   Argentina

2. Ecuador   _____   Venezuela

3. Peru   _____   Bolivia

4. Argentina   _____   Brazil

5. Montevideo, Uruguay   _____   Buenos Aires, Argentina

6. Madeira River   _____   Atlantic Ocean

7. Argentina   _____   Paraguay

8. Guyana   _____   French Guiana

9. Bolivia   _____   Brazil

10. Bahia Blanca   _____   Golfo San Jorge

11. Argentina   _____   Uruguay

12. Colombia   _____   Guyana

13. Rio Negro   _____   Madeira River

14. Guyana   _____   Peru

15. Pacific Ocean   _____   Atlantic Ocean

Make your own sandwich:

_____   _____   _____

WEB SITES OF
SOUTH AMERICA

If each country of South America had its own Web site, what would it be? Match the name of the country, island, or dependency of South America that goes with each of the following Web site addresses. (Note: These are not actual sites!)

1. www.quito.geo _____

2. www.brasilia.geo _____

3. www.georgetown.geo _____

4. www.buenosaires.geo _____

5. www.cayenne.geo _____

6. www.santiago.geo _____

7. www.bogota.geo _____

8. www.asuncion.geo _____

9. www.lima.geo _____

10. www.montevideo.geo _____

11. www.paramaribo.geo _____

12. www.caracas.geo _____

13. www.portofspain.geo _____

14. www.lapazsucre.geo _____

15. www.stanley.geo _____

SOUTH AMERICA DIRECTION CONNECTION

Look at a map of South America. Given the location of a particular country and a direction in which to go, determine the country that is your final destination.

1. From Uruguay go west to _____.

2. From Bolivia go north to _____.

3. From Ecuador go south to _____.

4. From Guyana go east to _____.

5. From Venezuela go west to _____.

6. From Uruguay go north to _____.

7. From Argentina go south to _____.

8. From Colombia go east to _____.

9. From Argentina go west to _____.

10. From Ecuador go north to _____.

11. From Trinidad & Tobago go south to _____.

12. From French Guiana go east to _____.

13. From Bolivia go west to _____.

14. From Paraguay go north to _____.

15. From French Guiana go south to _____.

16. From the Galapagos Islands go east to _____.

17. From the Falkland Islands go west to _____.

18. From Colombia go north to _____.

19. From Paraguay go south to _____.

20. From Suriname go east to _____.

SOUTH AMERICA
IN ABC ORDER

Picture yourself on the continent of South America. Look around. What do you see? Think of at least one sight you might see for each letter of the alphabet. List your brainstorms below. (Hint: Think of the different land areas, animals, and people.)

A _____

B _____

C _____

D _____

E _____

F _____

G _____

H _____

I _____

J _____

K _____

L _____

M _____

N _____

O _____

P _____

Q _____

R _____

S _____

T _____

U _____

V _____

W _____

X _____

Y _____

Z _____

MAP OF AFRICA

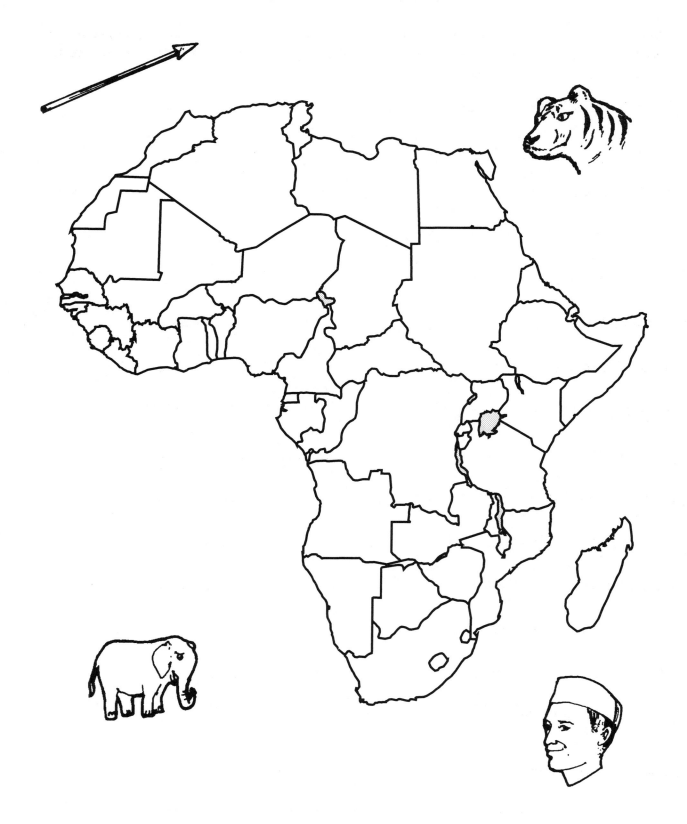

AFRICAN ANALOGIES – 1

Analogy puzzles are thinking games involving relationships between paired items. Finding the relationship between the given pair of the analogy will give you the key to solving the second pair. Use a map of Africa and reference books to solve these analogies.

1. Kenya:Indian Ocean::Liberia:_____

2. Kalahari:desert::Zambezi:_____

3. Chad:Libya::Namibia:_____

4. Lion:cub::elephant:_____

5. Congo:Brazzaville::Gabon:_____

6. Masai:_____::Berbers:Morocco

7. 20° S Latitude:Botswana::_____:Niger

8. Giraffe:tallest::_____:second tallest

9. Gambia:English::Congo:_____

10. Tunisia:Mediterranean Sea::Sudan:_____

11. Ghana:Togo::Liberia:_____

12. Mount Kilimanjaro:Tanzania::Victoria Falls:_____

13. Largest:Sudan::smallest:_____

14. Carnivore:hyena::herbivore:_____

15. Senegal:Dakar::Ethiopia:_____

Write your own African analogy:

_____:_____::_____:_____

AFRICAN ANALOGIES - 2

Analogy puzzles are thinking games involving relationships between paired items. Finding the relationship between the given pair of the analogy will give you the key to solving the second pair. Use a map of Africa and reference books to solve these analogies.

1. Congo River:_____::Zambezi River:Indian Ocean

2. Somalia:Gulf of Aden::Cameroon:_____

3. South Africa:Republic of South Africa::Morocco:_____

4. Algiers:Algeria::_____:Tunisia

5. Zimbabwe:Rhodesia::Namibia:_____

6. _____:Sierra Leone::Egypt:Sudan

7. Highest elevation:Mount Kilimanjaro::lowest elevation:_____

8. Cape Town:South Africa::_____:Rwanda

9. Ostrich:_____::cheetah:70 MPH

10. Zebra:mare::giraffe:_____

11. Zambia:Angola::_____:Zimbabwe

12. Rhinoceros:_____::hippopotamus:Hippopotamidae

13. Egypt:Arabic::Benin:_____

14. Sahara Desert:Algeria::Kalahari Desert:_____

15. Bull:elephant::_____:zebra

Write your own African analogy:

_____:_____::_____:_____

AFRICAN ANALOGIES - 3

Analogy puzzles are thinking games involving relationships between paired items. Finding the relationship between the given pair of the analogy will give you the key to solving the second pair. Use a map of Africa and reference books to solve these analogies.

1. Khartoum:Sudan::_____:Kenya

2. Hippopotamus:river::_____:savannah

3. Ethiopia:Somalia::_____:Congo

4. Tropic of Capricorn:Botswana::_____:Zaire

5. Ivory Coast:Abidjan::Libya:_____

6. Ostrich:_____::lion:lioness

7. Lake Nyasa:Malawi::Lake Nassar:_____

8. Togo:Benin::Western Sahara:_____

9. Baobab:_____::papyrus:water plant

10. Lualaba River:Zaire::Nile River:_____

11. Crocodile:reptile::gorilla:_____

12. Sao Tome & Principe:Atlantic Ocean::Madagascar:_____

13. Kinshasa:Zaire:Luanda:_____

14. Botswana:South Africa::Kenya:_____

15. Kampala:Uganda::_____:Egypt

Write your own African analogy:

_____:_____::_____:_____

WHICH ONE DOES NOT BELONG?

Listed below are groups of four items in categories such as rivers, lakes, etc. Three items in the group have something in common; the fourth item does not belong. Circle the item that does not belong and then tell why.

1. Guinea, Chad, South Africa, Somalia

   Why? _____

2. Elephant, lion, hyena, cheetah

   Why? _____

3. Uganda, Zimbabwe, Mali, Nigeria

   Why? _____

4. Ethiopia, Zaire, Mali, Madagascar

   Why? _____

5. Rhinoceros, camel, giraffe, hippopotamus

   Why? _____

6. Kalahari, Atlas, Sahara, Libyan

   Why? _____

7. Khartoum, Cairo, Tripoli, Alexandria

   Why? _____

8. Sao Tome, Principe, Somalia, Madagascar

   Why? _____

9. Giraffe, rhinoceros, hyena, impala

   Why? _____

10. Lion, ostrich, elephant, gorilla

    Why? _____

Write your own "Which one does not belong?"

_____   _____   _____   _____

Which one does not belong? _____

Why? _____

AFRICA GEOGRAPHY SANDWICHES

Sandwiches are made with two pieces of bread and a filling in the middle. In these geography sandwiches, you are given the "bread" but not the "filling." Study a globe or a map of the world to make a proper sandwich.

1. Morocco   _____   Tunisia

2. Egypt   _____   Uganda

3. Zaire   _____   Tanzania

4. Namibia   _____   Zimbabwe

5. Mauritania   _____   Ivory Coast

6. Mozambique   _____   Madagascar

7. Libya   _____   Central African Republic

8. Ghana   _____   Benin

9. Angola   _____   Zimbabwe

10. Sudan   _____   Somalia

11. Mediterranean Sea   _____   Gulf of Aden

12. Benin   _____   Cameroon

13. Gabon   _____   Zaire

14. Nigeria   _____   Chad

15. Sierra Leone   _____   Ivory Coast

Make your own sandwich:

_____   _____   _____

WEB SITES OF AFRICA

If each country of Africa had a Web site on the Internet, what might its address be? Read each address and find the country that might list itself in this way. (Note: These are not actual sites!)

1. www.cairo.geo _____

2. www.kinshasa.geo _____

3. www.bamako.geo _____

4. www.capetown.geo _____

5. www.yamoussoukro.geo _____

6. www.ndjamena.geo _____

7. www.luanda.geo _____

8. www.addisababa.geo _____

9. www.tripoli.geo _____

10. www.lusaka.geo _____

11. www.freetown.geo _____

12. www.rabat.geo _____

13. www.antananarivo.geo _____

14. www.kampala.geo _____

15. www.lome.geo _____

Write your own African Web site addresses:

_____ _____

AFRICA
DIRECTION CONNECTION

Look at a map of Africa. Given the location of a particular country and a direction in which to go, determine the country that is your final destination.

1. From Tunisia go west to _____.

2. From Equatorial Guinea go north to _____.

3. From Lesotho go south to _____.

4. From Togo go east to_____.

5. From Zambia go west to _____.

6. From Senegal go north to _____.

7. From Egypt go south to _____.

8. From Cameroon go west to _____.

9. From Rwanda go west to_____.

10. From Ghana go north to _____.

11. From Gambia go south to _____.

12. From Burundi go east to _____.

13. From Liberia go east to _____.

14. From Uganda go north to_____.

15. From Kenya go south to _____.

16. From Sudan go east to _____.

17. From Botswana go west to _____.

18. From Chad go north to_____.

19. From Botswana go south to_____.

20. From Kenya go east to _____.

AFRICA IN ABC ORDER

Picture yourself on the continent of Africa. Look around. What do you see? Think of at least one sight you might see for each letter of the alphabet. List your brainstorms below. (Hint: Think of the different land areas, animals, and people.)

A _____

B _____

C _____

D _____

E _____

F _____

G _____

H _____

I _____

J _____

K _____

L _____

M _____

N _____

O _____

P _____

Q _____

R _____

S _____

T _____

U _____

V _____

W _____

X _____

Y _____

Z _____

MAP OF EUROPE

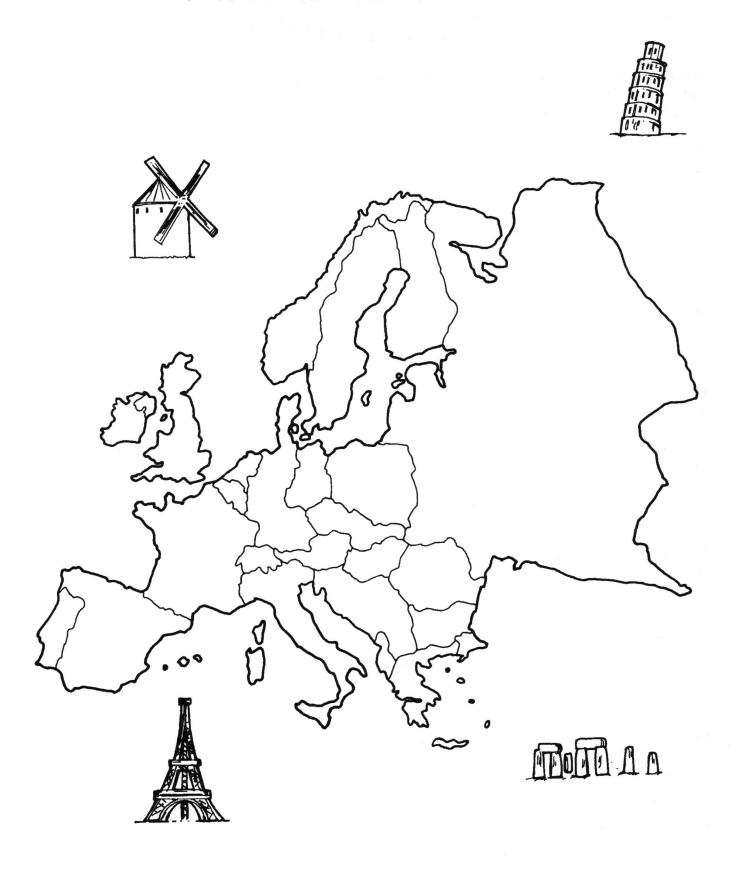

EUROPEAN ANALOGIES – 1

Analogy puzzles are thinking games involving relationships between paired items. Finding the relationship between the given pair of the analogy will give you the key to solving the second pair. Use a map of Europe and reference books to solve these analogies.

1. Stockholm:Sweden::_____:Belgium

2. Adriatic Sea:Italy::Aegean Sea:_____

3. Alps:Switzerland::Pyrenees:_____

4. Iceland:Atlantic Ocean::Sicily:_____

5. United Kingdom:Great Britain::Holland:_____

6. Rhine River:Germany::Thames River:_____

7. Stonehenge:England::Parthenon:_____

8. Beatrice Potter:Peter Rabbit::_____:Winnie-the-Pooh

9. Bulgaria:Yugoslavia::_____:Poland

10. Blue, white, and red:France::_____:Italy

11. Copenhagen:Denmark::_____:Poland

12. Baltic States:Estonia, Latvia and Lithuania::Scandinavia:_____

13. World War I:1914::World War II:_____

14. Big Ben:London::Arc de Triomphe:_____

15. Ferdinand V:Isabella::Napoleon I:_____

Write your own European analogy:

_____:_____::_____:_____

EUROPEAN ANALOGIES - 2

Analogy puzzles are thinking games involving relationships between paired items. Finding the relationship between the given pair of the analogy will give you the key to solving the second pair. Use a map of Europe and reference books to solve these analogies.

1. Lisbon:Portugal::Berlin:_____

2. Alexander Graham Bell:_____::Florence Nightingale:Italy

3. France:Mediterranean Sea::Norway:_____

4. Charles DeGaulle:France::Sir Winston Churchill:_____

5. Loch Ness:Scotland::Lake of Lucerne:_____

6. Queen Victoria:Prince Albert::Queen Elizabeth II:_____

7. Hungary:Budapest::Ireland:_____

8. Lithuania:Latvia::Belgium:_____

9. Mozart:_____::Michelangelo:Italy

10. 40° N Latitude:Portugal::_____:Sweden

11. Roman Catholic:Italy::_____:Scotland

12. River Shannon:_____::Vistula River:Poland

13. Ferdinand V: Spain::Henry VIII:_____

14. Finland:Helsinki::Netherlands:_____

15. Lira:Turkey::_____:Great Britain

Write your own European analogy:

_____:_____::_____:_____

EUROPEAN ANALOGIES - 3

Analogy puzzles are thinking games involving relationships between paired items. Finding the relationship between the given pair of the analogy will give you the key to solving the second pair. Use a map of Europe and reference books to solve these analogies.

1. Madrid:Spain::_____:Italy

2. Volga River:Caspian Sea::Danube River:_____

3. Charles Dickens:Portsmouth::William Shakespeare:_____

4. Christopher Columbus:Italy::Ferdinand Magellan:_____

5. France:Spain::_____:Bulgaria

6. Isle of Man:Irish Sea::Isle of Wight:_____

7. good-bye:English::_____:Italian

8. King Juan Carlos:Spain::Queen Elizabeth II:_____

9. Lyon:_____::Munich:Germany

10. Loch:lake::glen: _____

11. Vienna:Austria::_____:Greece

12. Lapps:Lapland::_____:Netherlands

13. Romania:Republica Romania::France:_____

14. Ebro River:Spain::Po River:_____

15. Thank you:English::_____:Spanish

Write your own European analogy:

_____:_____::_____:_____

WHICH ONE DOES NOT BELONG?

Listed below are groups of four items in categories such as rivers, lakes, etc. Three items in the group have something in common; the fourth item does not belong. Circle the item that does not belong and then tell why.

1. Cow, buffalo, horse, pig

   Why? _____

2. France, Italy, Czech Republic, Netherlands

   Why? _____

3. Berlin, Barcelona, London, Rome

   Why? _____

4. Greece, Spain, Ireland, Italy

   Why? _____

5. Norway, Denmark, Germany, Sweden

   Why? _____

6. Pyrenees, Alps, Appennines, Gibraltar

   Why? _____

7. Italy, Corsica, Sardinia, Sicily

   Why? _____

8. Portugal, Austria, England, France

   Why? _____

9. French, Spanish, Scotland, German

   Why? _____

10. Adriatic, Mediterranean, Baltic, Caspian

   Why? _____

Write your own "Which one does not belong?"

_____ _____ _____ _____

Which one does not belong? _____

Why? _____

EUROPE GEOGRAPHY SANDWICHES

Sandwiches are made with two pieces of bread and a filling in the middle. In these geography sandwiches, you are given the "bread" but not the "filling." Study a globe or a map of the world to make a proper sandwich.

1. Germany   _____   Belarus

2. France   _____   Spain

3. Switzerland   _____   Austria

4. England   _____   France

5. Europe   _____   Africa

6. Iceland   _____   Norway

7. Corsica   _____   Sardinia

8. Italy   _____   Croatia

9. Europe   _____   Asia

10. Sweden   _____   Poland

11. Greece   _____   Crete

12. England   _____   Denmark

13. Estonia   _____   Lithuania

14. Romania   _____   Bulgaria

15. Netherlands   _____   France

Make your own sandwich:

_____ _____ _____

WEB SITES OF EUROPE

If each major city in Europe had a Web site on the Internet, what might its address be? Read each address and find the country that might list its famous sites in this way. (Note: These are not actual sites!)

1. www.eiffel.geo _____

2. www.bigben.geo _____

3. www.bullfight.geo _____

4. www.parthenon.geo _____

5. www.redsquare.geo _____

6. www.dutch.geo _____

7. www.pizza.geo _____

8. www.alps.geo _____

9. www.blarneystone.geo _____

10. www.mozart.geo _____

11. www.fjord.geo _____

12. www.kilt.geo _____

13. www.grimms.geo _____

14. www.midnightsun.geo _____

15. www.nato.geo _____

Write your own European Web site addresses:

_____   _____

EUROPE DIRECTION CONNECTION

Look at a map of Europe. Given the location of a particular country and a direction in which to go, determine the country that is your final destination.

1. From Switzerland go west to _____.

2. From England go north to _____.

3. From Belarus go south to _____.

4. From the Netherlands go east to _____.

5. From Belgium go south to _____.

6. From Bulgaria go north to _____.

7. From Liechtenstein go south to _____.

8. From Ireland go east to _____.

9. From Sweden go west to _____.

10. From Lithuania go north to _____.

11. From Switzerland go south to _____.

12. From Portugal go east to _____.

13. From Moldova go west to _____.

14. From Spain go north to _____.

15. From Estonia go south to _____.

16. From Bosnia go west to _____.

17. From Finland go west to _____.

18. From Slovenia go north to _____.

19. From Denmark go south to _____.

20. From Macedonia go east to _____.

EUROPE IN ABC ORDER

Picture yourself on the continent of Europe. Look around. What do you see? Think of at least one sight you might see for each letter of the alphabet. List your brainstorms below. (Hint: Think of the different countries, man-made structures, and people.)

A _____

B _____

C _____

D _____

E _____

F _____

G _____

H _____

I _____

J _____

K _____

L _____

M _____

N _____

O _____

P _____

Q _____

R _____

S _____

T _____

U _____

V _____

W _____

X _____

Y _____

Z _____

MAP OF AUSTRALIA

AUSTRALIAN ANALOGIES – 1

Analogy puzzles are thinking games involving relationships between paired items. Finding the relationship between the given pair of the analogy will give you the key to solving the second pair. Use a map of Australia and reference books to solve these analogies.

1. Adelaide:South Australia::_____:Queensland

2. Geese:flock::kangaroo:_____

3. Great Victoria:desert::Nullarbor:_____

4. Wallaby:mammal::cassowary:_____

5. Victoria:New South Wales::New South Wales:_____

6. Tasmanian devil:carnivore::koala:_____

7. Shark Bay:Western Australia::Port Phillip Bay:_____

8. Bird:feathers::marsupial:_____

9. Outback:desert::Great Dividing Range:_____

10. Wellesley Island:Gulf of Carpentaria::King Island:_____

11. Queensland koala:endangered species::Tasmanian wolf:_____

12. Murchison River:Western Australia::Victoria River:_____

13. Male kangaroo:boomer::female kangaroo:_____

14. Lake Disappointment:_____::Lake Frome:South Australia

15. Kookaburra:bird::wallaby:_____

Write your own Australian analogy:

_____:_____::_____:_____

AUSTRALIAN ANALOGIES – 2

Analogy puzzles are thinking games involving relationships between paired items. Finding the relationship between the given pair of the analogy will give you the key to solving second pair. Use a map of Australia and reference books to solve these analogies.

1. Sydney:New South Wales::_____:Western Australia

2. Koala:tree:wombat:_____

3. Lake Eyre:South Australia::Lake Barlee:_____

4. Kangaroo:bears live young::platypus:_____

5. South Australia:Western Australia::Victoria:_____

6. Great Sandy:desert::Kimberley:_____

7. DeGray River:Western Australia::Dawson River:_____

8. Tasmanian wolf:Tasmanian tiger::koala:_____

9. Gulf of Carpentaria:Northern Territory and Queensland::
   Great Australian Bight:_____

10. Queensland:Coral Sea::New South Wales:_____

11. Kookaburra:bird::goanna:_____

12. MacDonnell Ranges:Northern Territory::Snowy Mountains:_____

13. Red kangaroo:desert::gray kangaroo:_____

14. Drysdale River National Park:Western Australia::
    Uluru National Park:_____

15. Botany Bay:New South Wales::Encounter Bay:_____

Write your own Australian analogy:

_____:_____::_____:_____

AUSTRALIAN ANALOGIES – 3

Analogy puzzles are thinking games involving relationships between paired items. Finding the relationship between the given pair of the analogy will give you the key to solving the second pair. Use a map of Australia and reference books to solve these analogies.

1. Hobart:Tasmania::_____:Victoria

2. Emu:bird::taipan:_____

3. Darling River:New South Wales::Ashburton River:_____

4. Koala:Phalangeridae::kangaroo:_____

5. New South Wales:Victoria::Northern Territory:_____

6. Kangaroo:_____::dingo:pup

7. Lake Eyre:lowest elevation::_____:highest elevation

8. Western Australia:Indian Ocean::Queensland:_____

9. Crocodile:_____::red kangaroo:herbivore

10. Melville Island:Northern Territory::Kangaroo Island:_____

11. Queensland koala:Queensland::Tasmanian devil:___ _____

12. Lake Gairdner:_____::Lake Gordon:Tasmania

13. Koala:eucalyptus leaves::kangaroo:_____

14. Simpson Desert National Park:Queensland::
    Randall River National Park:_____

15. Cape Leeuwin:Western Australia::Cape York:_____

Write your own Australian analogy:

_____:_____::_____:_____

WHICH ONE DOES NOT BELONG?

Listed below are groups of four items in categories such as rivers, lakes, etc. Three items in the group have something in common; the fourth item does not belong. Circle the item that does not belong and then tell why.

1. Queensland, Victoria, Sydney, Tasmania

   Why? _____

2. Perth, Gibson, Simpson, Great Victoria

   Why? _____

3. Hobart, Adelaide, Brisbane, Canberra

   Why? _____

4. Bass, Timor, Coral, Tasman

   Why? _____   _____

5. Koala, kangaroo, wombat, dingo

   Why? _____

6. Hamersley, Flinders, Nullarbor, Stuart

   Why? _____

7. Tasmania, Victoria, Queensland, New South Wales

   Why? _____

8. Sheep, wallaby, wallaroo, numbat

   Why? _____

9. Tasmania, Kangaroo, Cape York, Flinders

   Why? _____

10. Carpentaria, Shark, Port Phillip, Botany

    Why? _____

Write your own "Which one does not belong?"

_____   _____   _____   _____

Which one does not belong? _____

Why? _____

AUSTRALIA GEOGRAPHY SANDWICHES

Sandwiches are made with two pieces of bread and a filling in the middle. In these geography sandwiches, you are given the "bread" but not the "filling." Study a globe or a map of the world to make a proper sandwich.

1. Queensland _____ Western Australia

2. New Guinea _____ Australia

3. Cape Arnhem _____ Cape York

4. Outback _____ Pacific Ocean

5. Queensland _____ Victoria

6. Melbourne _____ Sydney

7. New South Wales _____ Victoria

8. Western Australia _____ New South Wales

9. South Australia _____ Indian Ocean

10. Victoria _____ Tasmania

11. Ashburton River _____ Murchison River

12. Western Australia _____ Victoria

13. Flinders River _____ Mitchell River

14. Coral Sea _____ Tasman Sea

15. Northern Territory _____ New South Wales

Make your own sandwich:

_____   _____   _____

WEB SITES OF AUSTRALIA

Australia, New Guinea, New Zealand, and other nearby islands make up the area known as Australasia. If each of the states, countries, and territories of Australasia had a Web site on the Internet, what would the addresses be? Read each address and find out what state or territory might list itself in this way. (Note: These are not actual sites!)

1. www.adelaide.geo _____

2. www.portmoresby.geo _____

3. www.brisbane.geo _____

4. www.canberra.geo _____

5. www.wellington.geo _____

6. www.perth.geo _____

7. www.jakarta.geo _____

8. www.hobart.geo _____

9. www.darwin.geo _____

10. www.kualalumpur.geo _____

11. www.sydney.geo _____

12. www.melbourne.geo _____

Write your own Australian Web site addresses:

_____ _____

AUSTRALIA
DIRECTION CONNECTION

Look at a map of Australia. Given the location of a particular state and a direction in which to go, determine your final destination.

1. From the Northern Territory go west to _____.

2. From Tasmania go north to _____.

3. From New South Wales go south to _____.

4. From the Northern Territory go east to _____.

5. From South Australia go west to _____.

6. From New South Wales go north to _____.

7. From Victoria go south to_____.

8. From Western Australia go east to _____.

9. From New South Wales go west to _____.

10. From Victoria go north to _____.

11. From the Northern Territory go south to _____.

12. From South Australia go east to _____.

13. From Victoria go west to _____.

14. From South Australia go north to_____.

15. From Queensland go south to _____.

AUSTRALIA IN ABC ORDER

Picture yourself on the continent of Australia. Look around. What do you see? Think of at least one sight you might see for each letter of the alphabet. List your brainstorms below. (Hint: Think of the different land areas, animals, and people.)

A _____

B _____

C _____

D _____

E _____

F _____

G _____

H _____

I _____

J _____

K _____

L _____

M _____

N _____

O _____

P _____

Q _____

R _____

S _____

T _____

U _____

V _____

W _____

X _____

Y _____

Z _____

MAP OF ASIA

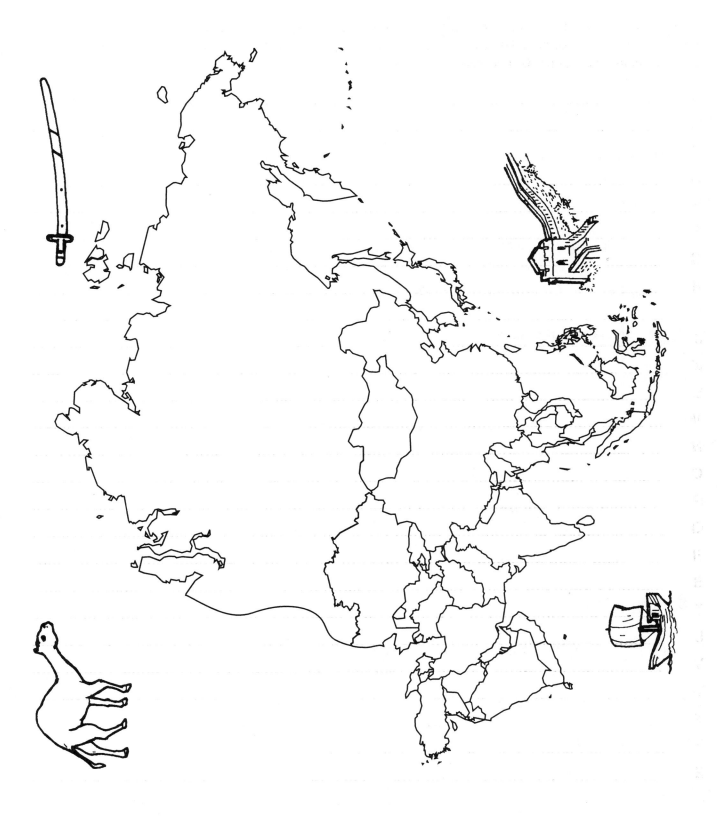

ASIAN ANALOGIES – 1

Analogy puzzles are thinking games involving relationships between paired items. Finding the relationship between the given pair of the analogy will give you the key to solving the second pair. Use a map of Asia and reference books to solve these analogies.

1. Kabul:Afghanistan::Vientiane:_____

2. Yemen:Gulf of Aden::Pakistan:_____

3. North Korea:South Korea::Lebanon:_____

4. Teheran:Iran::_____:United Arab Emirates

5. Malaysia:peninsula::Sumatra:_____

6. Yangtze River:China::Ganges River:_____

7. Yemen:Saudi Arabia::Nepal:_____

8. Turkey:Black Sea::Iran:_____

9. Islamabad:_____::Seoul:South Korea

10. Euphrates River:_____::Ural River:Caspian Sea

11. Mongolia:China::Syria:_____

12. Japan:Japanese::Lebanon:_____

13. Eiffel Towel:France::Taj Mahal:_____

14. Dead Sea:Israel and Jordan::Mount Everest:_____

15. _____:Mongolia::Tokyo:Japan

Write your own Asian analogy:

_____:_____::_____:_____

ASIAN ANALOGIES – 2

Analogy puzzles are thinking games involving relationships between paired items. Finding the relationship between the given pair of the analogy will give you the key to solving the second pair. Use a map of Asia and reference books to solve these analogies.

1. Damascus:Syria::New Delhi:_____

2. Japan:island::South Korea:_____

3. Bangladesh:Bay of Bengal::Kuwait:_____

4. Afghanistan:_____::Nepal:India

5. Dhaka:Bangladesh::_____:Vietnam

6. Indus River:Pakistan::Tigris River:_____

7. Turkmenistan:Uzbekistan::Yemen:_____

8. Sana:Yemen::Riyadh:_____

9. Cyprus:Mediterranean Sea::Sri Lanka:_____

10. India:prime minister::Oman:_____

11. _____:China::Baghdad:Iraq

12. Ganges River:Bay of Bengal::Yangtze River:_____

13. Gulf of Oman:Arabian Sea::Bay of Bengal:_____

14. Ganges:river::Gobi:_____

15. _____:Lebanon::Columbo:Sri Lanka

Write your own Asian analogy:

_____:_____::_____:_____

ASIAN ANALOGIES – 3

Analogy puzzles are thinking games involving relationships between paired items. Finding the relationship between the given pair of the analogy will give you the key to solving the second pair. Use a map of Asia and reference books to solve these analogies.

1. Rangoon:Myanmar::Jerusalem:_____

2. Taiwan:East China Sea::Luzon:_____

3. Ob River:Russia::Huang He River:_____

4. Syria:Turkey::Kyrgyzstan:_____

5. Kathmandu:Nepal::_____:Taiwan

6. Saudi Arabia:Red Sea::_____:Sea of Japan

7. Xi Jiang River:South China Sea::Indus River:_____

8. Sea of Japan:Yellow Sea::East China Sea:_____

9. Dromedary camel:domesticated::reindeer:_____

10. Bangkok:_____::Muscat:Oman

11. Tajikistan:China::Cambodia:_____

12. Komodo dragon:Komodo Island::orangutan:_____

13. Manila:Philippines::Phnom Penh:_____

14. Kyzylkum:desert::Himalayas:_____

15. _____:Jordan::Ankara:Turkey

Write your own Asian analogy:

_____:_____::_____:_____

WHICH ONE DOES NOT BELONG?

Listed below are groups of four items in categories such as rivers, lakes, etc. Three items in the group have something in common; the fourth item does not belong. Circle the item that does not belong and then tell why.

1. Pakistan, Nepal, Vietnam, China

   Why? _____

2. Cambodia, Japan, Sri Lanka, Taiwan

   Why? _____

3. Beijing, Kabul, Teheran, Bombay

   Why? _____

4. Gobi, Tigris, Euphrates, Ganges

   Why? _____

5. Turkey, Saudi Arabia, Israel, Syria

   Why? _____

6. Tiger, camel, panda, llama

   Why? _____

7. Arabian, South China, Aden, Yellow

   Why? _____

8. Iran, India, Iraq, Saudi Arabia

   Why? _____

9. South Korea, Afghanistan, Mongolia, Bhutan

   Why? _____

10. Capsian, Zagros, Himalayas, Altai

    Why? _____

Write your own "Which one does not belong?"

_____   _____   _____   _____

Which one does not belong? _____

Why? _____

ASIA GEOGRAPHY SANDWICHES

Sandwiches are made with two pieces of bread and a filling in the middle. In these geography sandwiches, you are given the "bread" but not the "filling." Study a map of Asia to make a proper sandwich.

1. Syria _____ Iran

2. India _____ China

3. Oman _____ Pakistan

4. Kuwait _____ Yemen

5. Thailand _____ India

6. Vietnam _____ Philippines

7. North Korea _____ Japan

8. Israel _____ Saudi Arabia

9. Indonesia _____ India

10. Turkmenistan _____ Pakistan

11. Thailand _____ Laos

12. India _____ Thailand

13. South Korea _____ Taiwan

14. Afghanistan _____ India

15. Turkey _____ Azerbaijan

Make your own sandwich:

_____   _____   _____

WEB SITES OF ASIA

If each country in Asia had a Web site on the Internet, what might its address be? Read each address and find out what country might list itself in this way. (Note: These are not actual sites!)

1. www.bangkok.geo   _____

2. www.ulanbator.geo   _____

3. www.riyadh.geo   _____

4. www.islamabad.geo   _____

5. www.dhaka.geo   _____

6. www.beijing.geo   _____

7. www.seoul.geo   _____

8. www.tehran.geo   _____

9. www.jerusalem.geo   _____

10. www.hanoi.geo   _____

11. www.newdelhi.geo   _____

12. www.tokyo.geo   _____

13. www.amman.geo   _____

14. www.ankara.geo   _____

15. www.damascus.geo   _____

Write your own Asian Web site addresses:

_____ _____

ASIA DIRECTION CONNECTION

Look at a map of Asia. Given the location of a particular country and a direction in which to go, determine your final destination.

1. From Afghanistan go west to _____.

2. From Nepal go north to _____.

3. From Jordan go south to _____.

4. From Yemen go east to _____.

5. From Thailand go west to _____.

6. From Uzbekistan go north to _____.

7. From Israel go east to _____.

8. From South Korea go east to _____.

9. From Bangladesh go west to _____.

10. From Kuwait go north to _____.

11. From Afghanistan go south to _____.

12. From Laos go east to _____.

13. From North Korea go west to _____.

14. From Syria go north to _____.

15. From Mongolia go south to _____.

16. From Syria go east to _____.

17. From Cambodia go west to _____.

18. From Bhutan go north to _____.

19. From Iraq go south to _____.

20. From Turkmenistan go east to _____.

ASIA IN
ABC ORDER

Picture yourself on the continent of Asia. Look around? What do you see? Think of at least one sight you might see for each letter of the alphabet. List your brainstorms below. (Hint: Think of the different countries, animals, and people.)

A _____

B _____

C _____

D _____

E _____

F _____

G _____

H _____

I _____

J _____

K _____

L _____

M _____

N _____

O _____

P _____

Q _____

R _____

S _____

T _____

U _____

V _____

W _____

X _____

Y _____

Z _____

ANSWER KEY

Page 6
1. Canberra, capital: country
2. Africa, country: continent
3. South America, native bird: continent
4. Mediterranean Sea, delta: location
5. Aborigines, native people: continent
6. Northern territory, geographic location
7. Mount Kosciusko, tallest mountain: continent
8. Nile River, dam: location
9. pride, animal: name for group
10. Mississippi River, longest river: continent
11. president, head of government: country
12. Africa, largest lake: continent
13. Asia, country: continent
14. joey, animal: name for young
15. Asia, native animal: continent

Page 7
1. Ottawa, capital: country
2. Asia, country: continent
3. Australia, native animal: continent
4. Africa, cape: continent
5. Dutch, official language: country
6. South America, geographic location
7. Aconcagua, tallest mountain: continent
8. Indian Ocean, island: location
9. dingo, prey: predator
10. Murray River, longest river: continent
11. Italy, geographic location
12. North America, desert: continent
13. France/Spain, bay: bordering country
14. Asia, native animal: continent
15. Asia, islands: nearest continent

Page 8
1. Mexico City, capital: country
2. Australia, country: continent
3. China, Tibet, or Asia, native animal: country or continent
4. Paris, museum: location
5. "Advance Australia Fair," national anthem: country
6. Atlantic and Pacific Oceans, canal: connecting bodies of water
7. Mount Kilimanjaro, tallest mountain: continent

8. Africa, mountain range: continent
9. Australia, native animal: continent
10. South America, longest river: continent
11. Tasmania, smallest-largest state
12. Egypt, prehistoric building: country
13. Himalayas, mountain: range
14. Italy, volcano: location
15. South America, country: continent

Page 9
1. Turkey, not a country in Africa
2. India, not an island
3. Alaska, not a country in North America
4. Mediterranean, not an ocean
5. Chad, does not border the Mediterranean Sea
6. Canary, islands not located in the Pacific Ocean
7. Antarctica, continent with no inhabitants
8. New Zealand, not a state in Australia
9. South Africa, country not bisected by the equator
10. Angola, does not border the Indian Ocean or Australia, only country that is also a continent

Page 10
1. Atlantic Ocean
2. Equator
3. Tasman Sea
4. Ural Mountains
5. Indian Ocean
6. Central America
7. Prime Meridian
8. Indian Ocean
9. Mediterranean Sea
10. Pacific Ocean
11. Atlantic Ocean
12. Equator
13. Red Sea/Indian Ocean
14. Drake Passage
15. Pacific Ocean

Page 11
1. France
2. Germany
3. Mexico
4. France
5. Italy
6. Netherlands
7. Spain & California
8. Germany
9. Pennsylvania

10. England
11. South America
12. England
13. France
14. Border of Europe & Asia
15. England

Page 12
1. peso
2. dollar
3. rand
4. pound
5. franc
6. mark
7. drachma
8. rupee
9. yen
10. lira
11. peseta
12. shekel
13. schilling
14. won
15. balboa
16. bolivar
17. guilder
18. ruble
19. markka
20. krona

Page 13
North America: bison, coyote, Kodiak bear, northern raccoon, skunk
Europe: fallow deer, nightingale, Norway lemming, pine marten, Pyrenean ibex
Asia: Bengal tiger, camel, cobra, orangutan, panda
South America: anaconda, llama, rhea, sloth, spectacled bear
Africa: cheetah, elephant, giraffe, lion, ostrich
Australia: kangaroo, koala, numbat, Tasmanian devil, wombat

Page 14
Accept place names that may be found in states other than those listed.
1. New York City, New York
2. Cambridge, Massachusetts
3. Lincoln, Nebraska
4. Plymouth, Massachusetts
5. Salisbury, Maryland
6. Reading, Massachusetts
7. New Bern, North Carolina
8. Birmingham, Alabama
9. Rome, Georgia
10. Paris, Texas
11. St. Petersburg, Florida
12. Manchester, New Hampshire
13. Athens, Georgia
14. Valencia, California
15. New Orleans, Louisiana
16. Waterloo, Iowa
17. Memphis, Tennessee
18. Odessa, Texas
19. Cleveland, Ohio
20. Frankfort, Kentucky

Page 15
Africa: Nile River/4,145 miles/Mediterranean Sea
South America: Amazon

River/4,000 miles/Atlantic Ocean
Asia: Yangtze River/3,915 miles/East China Sea
North America: Mississippi River/2,340 miles/Gulf of Mexico
Europe: Volga River/2,194 miles/Caspian Sea
Australia: Murray River/1,609 miles/Tasman Sea
Asia: Mount Everest/29,028 feet/Nepal-Tibet Border
South America: Aconagua/22,831 feet/ Argentina
North America: Mount McKinley/ 20,320 feet/USA
Africa: Mount Kilimanjaro/ 19,390 feet/Tanzania
Europe: Mount Elbrus/18,481 feet/Russia
Antarctica: Vinson Massif/ 16,864 feet/ Antarctica
Australia: Mount Kosciusko/ 7,310 feet/Australia

Page 16
1. Greece, Europe, 200 BC
2. Iraq, Asia, 600-550 BC
3. Egypt, Africa, 2500 BC
4. Greece, Europe, 435 BC
5. Turkey, Europe, 350 BC
6. Egypt, Africa, 270 BC
7. Greece, Europe, 550 BC
First to last: Pyramids of Giza, Hanging Gardens of Babylon, Temple of Artemis, Statue of Zeus, Mausoleum at Halicarnassus, Colossus of Rhodes, Lighthouse of Alexandria.

Page 17 Answers will vary.
Page 19
1. Alabama, geographic location
2. Delaware, state: order of admission to Union
3. Yale, U.S. president: college attended
4. Gulf of Mexico, river: mouth
5. Bismarck, capital: state
6. Apache, Native American: tribe
7. U.S.A., state: country
8. 26, U.S. president: presidency number
9. Pacific Ocean, ocean: bordering state
10. Arizona, national park: location
11. Mississippi River, river: bordering state

ANSWER KEY (cont.)

12. Canada, state/province: country
13. Empire State, state: nickname
14. copper, monument: construction material
15. Mexico, tribe: location

Page 20
1. 1803, state: year admitted to Union
2. four, U.S. president: years served
3. Lt. Governor, first and second in command
4. Canada, state: foreign country it borders
5. Minnesota, geographic location
6. Whig, U.S. president: party affiliation
7. Kentucky, national park: location
8. Providence, state: capital
9. Pennsylvania, river: location
10. 1889, state: year admitted to Union
11. Methodist, U.S. president: religious affiliation
12. six, office: term of office
13. 1917, U.S. president: year of birth
14. redwood, state tree: state
15. Columbus, capital: state

Page 21
1. Hunkpapa, Native American: band (not to be confused with tribe)
2. Palmetto State, state: nickname
3. "Bess" or Elizabeth, U.S. President: wife
4. New Mexico, geographic location
5. Powhatan, Native American: father
6. Caldwell, NJ, U.S. president: place of birth
7. Topeka, capital: state
8. Navajo, dwelling: Native American tribe
9. Andrew Johnson, assassinated U.S. president: vice president assuming office
10. sugar maple, state:state tree
11. Oklahoma, nickname: state
12. Lincoln, capital: state
13. Lake Erie, Great Lake: bordering state
14. Ottawa, national capital: country

15. Mayflower, European travelers: ship

Page 22
1. Mexico, not a river
2. Kansas, not on west coast
3. Utah, does not touch a Great Lake
4. Houston, not a state capital
5. Alaska, not a Canadian province
6. New Mexico, does not touch the Mississippi River
7. North Dakota, state with no coastline
8. Michigan, lake does not border Canada; also only lake with a state name in common
9. Kentucky, not a western state, only state east of the Mississippi River
10. North Carolina, state does not border a foreign country

Page 23
1. Alabama
2. South Dakota
3. Lake Michigan
4. Connecticut
5. Red River
6. Nevada
7. Rio Grande River
8. Indiana
9. New Mexico
10. Mississippi River
11. U.S.A.
12. New Hampshire
13. Iowa
14. California
15. Oregon

Page 24
1. Oaxaca
2. Gulf of California
3. Coahuila
4. Mexico
5. Zacatecas
6. Gulf of Mexico
7. Nayarit
8. Rio Grande River
9. Campeche
10. Queretaro
11. Isla Maria Magdelena
12. Sinaloa
13. Durango
14. Puebla
15. Guanajuato

Page 25
1. Monitoba, Canada
2. Nevada, U.S.A.
3. New York, U.S.A.
4. Louisiana, U.S.A.
5. Montana, U.S.A.

6. North Carolina, U.S.A.
7. Alberta, Canada
8. Alaska, U.S.A.
9. Texas, U.S.A.
10. Sonora, Mexico
11. Oregon, U.S.A.
12. Ontario, Canada
13. New Mexico, U.S.A.
14. Durango, Mexico
15. Maine, U.S.A.
16. Nuevo Leon, Mexico
17. British Columbia, Canada
18. California, U.S.A.
19. New Hampshire, U.S.A.
20. Tamaulipas, Mexico

Page 26
1. Arizona
2. Wyoming
3. Texas
4. Colorado
5. Kentucky
6. Oregon
7. Florida
8. Alaska
9. California
10. Arkansas
11. Hawaii
12. Washington
13. South Dakota
14. Virginia
15. New Mexico

Page 27
1. Colorado
2. Missouri
3. Florida
4. Minnesota
5. Utah
6. Montana
7. Massachusetts
8. Alabama
9. Tennessee
10. Michigan
11. Nebraska
12. Rhode Island
13. California
14. Tennessee
15. Texas
16. Georgia/Alabama
17. Arizona
18. Nebraska
19. Maryland
20. New Hampshire

Page 28
1. Monroe
2. Jefferson
3. Lincoln
4. Cleveland
5. Harrison
6. Johnson
7. Adams
8. Grant
9. Taylor
10. Clinton
11. Washington
12. Van Buren
13. Tyler
14. Madison
15. Jackson
16. Nixon
17. Polk
18. Coolidge
19. Roosevelt
20. Truman

Page 29
1. Land of Lincoln, Springfield
2. Beehive State, Salt Lake City
3. Mountain State, Charleston
4. Lone Star State, Austin

5. Wolverine State, Lansing
6. First State, Dover
7. Bluegrass State, Frankfort
8. Last Frontier, Juneau
9. Green Mountain State, Montpelier
10. Ocean State and Little Rhody, Providence
11. Flickertail State, Bismarck
12. Empire State, Albany
13. Empire State of the South, Atlanta
14. Volunteer State, Nashville
15. Badger State, Madison
16. Sunflower State, Topeka
17. Hoosier State, Indianapolis
18. Constitution State, Hartford
19. Evergreen State, Olympia
20. Golden State, Sacramento
21. Land of Enchantment, Santa Fe
22. Gopher State, St. Paul
23. Keystone State, Harrisburg
24. Magnolia State, Jackson
25. Equality State, Cheyenne

Page 30 Answers will vary.

Page 32
1. Bogota, capital: country
2. Atlantic Ocean, country: bordering ocean
3. Argentina, geographic location
4. Peru and Brazil, river: location
5. mammal, animal: group
6. Iguacu River, falls: location
7. Dutch, country: official language
8. Port of Spain, capital: country
9. Republica del Ecuador, country: official name
10. Chile, geographic location
11. peso, country: basic unit of money
12. cruzeiro, country: basic unit of money
13. camel, animal: family
14. Venezuela, peninsula: location
15. mammal, animal: group

Page 33
1. Paramaribo, capital: country
2. Argentina, gulf: bordering country
3. Chile, geographic location
4. reptile, animal: group
5. Peru, river: location
6. Atlantic Ocean, country: bordering ocean

7. Portuguese, country: official language
8. Georgetown, capital: country
9. Republica Oriental del Uruguay, country: official name
10. Argentina, islands: nearest country
11. guilder, country: basic unit of money
12. Equator, global line: intersecting country
13. carnivore, animal: group
14. Brazil, river: location
15. plants, animal: food it eats

Page 34
1. Lima, capital: country
2. Pacific Ocean, islands: location
3. Ecuador, geographic location
4. Brazil, river: location
5. mammal, animal: group
6. Argentina, mountain: location
7. English, country: official language
8. Venezuela, capital: country
9. Republic del Peru, country: official name
10. Bolivia, lake: location
11. sucre, country: basic unit of money
12. Atlantic Ocean, country: bordering ocean
13. bird, animal: group
14. Ecuador, gulf: bordering country
15. Galapagos Islands, animal: habitat

Page 35
1. Costa Rica, not on the continent of South America
2. Tocantins River, not a tributary of the Amazon
3. Bolivia, not bisected by the equator
4. rhea, bird, not a mammal
5. Ecuador, does not border the Atlantic Ocean
6. Rio de Janero, not a capital city
7. ostrich, not a South American animal
8. Maracaibo, not a river
9. Ecuador, not an island,
10. Paraguay, does not have a coastline

Page 36
1. Andes Mountains
2. Colombia

3. Lake Titicaca
4. Bolivia, Paraguay, or Uruguay
5. Rio de la Plata
6. Amazon River
7. Pilcomayo River
8. Suriname
9. Guapore River
10. Golfo San Matias
11. Uruguay River
12. Venezuela
13. Amazon River
14. Brazil
15. South America

Page 37
1. Ecuador
2. Brazil
3. Guyana
4. Argentina
5. French Guiana
6. Chile
7. Colombia
8. Paraguay
9. Peru
10. Uruguay
11. Suriname
12. Venezuela
13. Trinidad and Tobago
14. Bolivia
15. Falkland Islands

Page 38
1. Argentina
2. Brazil
3. Peru
4. Suriname
5. Columbia
6. Brazil/Venezuela
7. Chile
8. Brazil
9. Chile
10. Columbia
11. Venezuela
12. Brazil
13. Peru/Chile
14. Bolivia/Brazil
15. Brazil
16. Ecuador
17. Argentina
18. Venezuela
19. Argentina
20. French Guiana

Page 39 Answers will vary.

Page 41
1. Atlantic Ocean, country: bordering ocean
2. river, place name: geographic feature
3. Angola, geographic location
4. calf, animal: name for young
5. Libreville, country: capital
6. Kenya, native people: country

7. 20° N Latitude, global location: country
8. elephant, height compared to other animals
9. French, country: official language
10. Red Sea, country: bordering sea
11. Ivory Coast, country: geographic location
12. Zimbabwe/Zambia, physical feature: location
13. Sao Tome and Principe, country: rank in size on African continent
14. hippo, giraffe, or elephant group: animal (accept any plant eating African animal)
15. Addis Ababa, country: capital

Page 42
1. Atlantic Ocean, river: mouth
2. Gulf of Guinea, country: bordering gulf
3. Kingdom of Morocco, country: official name
4. Tunis, capital: country
5. South West Africa, country: former name
6. Guinea, geographic location
7. Lake Assal, highest-lowest elevation in Africa
8. Kigali, capital: country
9. 40 MPH, animal: rate of speed it can reach
10. cow, animal: name for female
11. Mozambique, geographic location
12. Rhinocerotidae, animal: scientific classification
13. French, country: official language
14. Botswana, Namibia, or South Africa, desert:location
15. stallion, male name: animal

Page 43
1. Nairobi, capital: country
2. giraffe, rhino, or lion, animal: habitat (accept any savanna animal)
3. Gabon, geographic location
4. Equator, line on globe: intersecting country
5. Tripoli, country: capital
6. hen, animal: name for female
7. Egypt, lake: location
8. Muaritania, geographic location
9. tree, African plant: group
10. Egypt/Sudan, river: location

11. mammal, animal: group
12. Indian Ocean, island: location
13. Angola, capital: country
14. Tanzania, geographic location
15. Cairo, capital: country

Page 44
1. Chad, country with no coastline
2. elephant, not a carnivore
3. Nigeria, country with a coastline
4. Madagascar, island country
5. camel, not a native animal/ not a savanna animal
6. Atlas, mountain range/not a desert
7. Alexandria, not a capital city
8. Somalia, not an island
9. hyena, not a herbivore
10. ostrich, bird/not a mammal or gorilla, not a savanna animal

Page 45
1. Algeria
2. Sudan
3. Lake Tanganyika
4. Botswana
5. Mali
6. Mozambique Channel
7. Chad
8. Togo
9. Zambia
10. Ethiopia
11. Red Sea
12. Nigeria
13. Congo
14. Lake Chad/Cameroon
15. Liberia/Guinea

Page 46
1. Egypt
2. Zaire
3. Mali
4. South Africa
5. Ivory Coast
6. Chad
7. Angola
8. Ethiopia
9. Libya
10. Zambia
11. Sierra Leone
12. Morocco
13. Madagascar
14. Uganda
15. Togo

Page 47
1. Algeria   11. Senegal
2. Cameroon   12. Tanzania
3. South Africa 13. Ivory Coast
4. Benin   14. Sudan

ANSWER KEY *(cont.)*

5. Angola
6. Mauritania
7. Sudan
8. Nigeria
9. Zaire
10. Burkina
15. Tanzania
16. Ethiopia
17. Namibia
18. Libya
19. South Africa
20. Somalia

Page 48 Answers will vary.

Page 50
1. Brussels, capital: country
2. Greece, sea: bordering country
3. France/Spain, mountain range: location
4. Mediterranean Sea, island: location
5. Netherlands, country: another name it is known by
6. England, river: location (accept Great Britain or United Kingdom)
7. Greece, ancient structure: location
8. Alan Milne, author: character from book
9. Ukraine/Belarus: geographic location
10. green/white/red, colors of flag: country
11. Warsaw, capital: country
12. Denmark, Norway, and Sweden, group name: countries
13. 1939, war: year it began
14. Paris, landmark: location
15. Josephine, famous European: wife

Page 51
1. Germany, capital: country
2. Scotland, famous person: country of birth
3. North Sea, country: bordering sea
4. Great Britain, leader: country
5. Switzerland, lake: location
6. Prince Phillip, queen: husband
7. Dublin, country: capital
8. Netherlands, geographic location
9. Austria, artist: country of birth
10. 60° N Latitude, line on globe: intersecting country
11. Church of Scotland or Presbyterian, main religion: country
12. Ireland, river: location
13. England, king: country
14. Amsterdam, country: capital

15. pound, basic unit of money: country

Page 52
1. Rome, capital: country
2. Black Sea, river: mouth
3. Stratford-on-Avon, author: place of birth
4. Portugal, explorer: country of birth
5. Romania, geographic location
6. English Channel, island: location
7. arrivaderci, term: language
8. England, monarch: country
9. France, city: location
10. valley, Scottish term: meaning
11. Athens, capital: country
12. Dutch, people: country (Accept Hollanders or Nederlanders)
13. Republique du France, country: official name
14. Italy, river: location
15. gracias, term: language

Page 53
1. buffalo, not a native animal
2. Czech Republic, country without a coastline
3. Barcelona, not a capital city
4. Ireland, does not border the Mediterranean Sea
5. Germany, not a Scandinavian country
6. Gibraltar, not a mountain range
7. Italy, not an island
8. Austria, does not border the Atlantic
9. Scotland, not a European language
10. Caspian, not a sea in Europe

Page 54
1. Poland
2. Pyrenees Mountains
3. Liechtenstein
4. English Channel
5. Mediterranean Sea
6. Norwegian Sea
7. Strait of Bonifacio
8. Adriatic Sea
9. Ural Mountains
10. Baltic Sea
11. Sea of Crete
12. North Sea
13. Latvia
14. Danube River
15. Belgium

Page 55
1. Paris, France
2. London, England
3. Madrid, Spain or Lisbon, Portugal
4. Athens, Greece
5. Moscow, Russia
6. Amsterdam, Netherlands
7. Rome, Italy
8. Bern, Switzerland or Vienna, Austria
9. Cork, Ireland
10. Vienna, Austria
11. Oslo, Norway
12. Edinburgh, Scotland
13. Berlin, Germany
14. Oslo, Norway or Helsinki, Finland
15. Brussels, Belgium

Page 56
1. France
2. Scotland
3. Ukraine
4. Germany
5. France/England Lux
6. Romania
7. Switzerland
8. England
9. Norway
10. Latvia
11. Italy
12. Spain
13. Romania
14. France
15. Latvia
16. Yugoslavia
17. Sweden
18. Austria
19. Germany
20. Bulgaria or Greece

Page 57 Answers will vary.

Page 59
1. Brisbane, capital: state
2. mob, herd, or troop, animal: name for group
3. plain, place name: geographic feature
4. bird, animal: group
5. Queensland, geographic location
6. herbivore, animal: group
7. Victoria, bay: location
8. pouch, animal: characteristic
9. mountains, place name: geographic feature
10. Bass Strait, island: location
11. extinct, animal: classification
12. Northern Territory, river: location
13. doe or flier animal: other name it is called

14. Western Australia, lake: location
15. marsupial, animal: group

Page 60
1. Perth, capital: state
2. burrow, animal: habitat
3. Western Australia, lake: location
4. lays eggs, animal: characteristic
5. South Australia, geographic location
6. plateau, place name: description
7. Queensland, river: location
8. native bear, animal: other name that animal is known by
9. Western Australia and South Australia, gulf: bordering states
10. Tasman Sea, state: bordering sea
11. reptile, animal: group
12. Victoria or New South Wales, mountains: location
13. forest, animal: habitat
14. Northern Territory, national park: location
15. South Australia, bay: location

Page 61
1. Melbourne, capital: state
2. reptile or snake, animal: group
3. Western Australia, river: location
4. Macropodidae, animal: scientific classification (macro-big, pod-foot)
5. South Australia, geographic location
6. joey, animal: name for young
7. Mount Kosciusko, geographic location: elevation
8. South Pacific Ocean, state: bordering ocean
9. carnivore, animal: group
10. South Australia, island: nearest state
11. Tasmania, animal: state where it is found
12. South Australia lake: location
13. grass/small plants, animal: food it eats
14. Western Australia, national park: location
15. Queensland, cape: location

ANSWER KEY (cont.)

Page 62
1. Sydney, not an Australian state
2. Perth, not a desert
3. Canberra, not a state capital
4. Bass, not a sea
5. dingo, not a marsupial or not a herbivore
6. Nullarbor, not a mountain range
7. Tasmania, only island state
8. sheep, not a native animal or not a marsupial
9. Cape York, not an island
10. Carpentaria, not a bay

Page 63
1. South Australia/Northern Territory
2. Great Barrier Reef/Coral Sea
3. Gulf of Carpentaria
4. Great Dividing Range
5. New South Wales
6. Canberra
7. Murray River
8. South Australia
9. Great Australian Bight
10. Bass Strait
11. Gascoyne River
12. South Australia
13. Gilbert River
14. Pacific Ocean
15. South Australia/Queensland

Page 64
1. South Australia
2. Papua New Guinea
3. Queensland
4. Australia
5. New Zealand
6. Western Australia
7. Indonesia
8. Tasmania
9. Northern Territory
10. Malaysia
11. New South Wales
12. Victoria

Page 65
1. Western Australia
2. Victoria
3. Victoria
4. Queensland
5. Western Australia
6. Queensland
7. Tasmania
8. South Australia/Northern Territory
9. South Australia
10. New South Wales
11. South Australia
12. Queensland, New South Wales, or Victoria
13. South Australia

14. Queensland/Northern Territory
15. New South Wales

Page 66 Answers will vary.

Page 68
1. Laos, capital: country
2. Gulf of Oman, country: bordering gulf
3. Israel, geographic location
4. Abu Dhabi, capital: country
5. island, country: geographic description
6. India, river: location
7. China, geographic location
8. Caspian Sea, country: bordering sea
9. Pakistan, capital: country
10. Persian Gulf, river: mouth
11. Turkey, geographic location
12. Arabic, country: official language
13. India, famous structure: location
14. Nepal/Tibet, highest and lowest elevation: location
15. Ulan Bator, capital: country

Page 69
1. India, capital: country
2. peninsula, country: geographic description
3. Persian Gulf, country: bordering body of water
4. Pakistan, geographic location
5. Hanoi, capital: country
6. Iraq/Turkey, river: location
7. Oman, geographic location
8. Saudi Arabia, capital: country
9. Indian Ocean, island: location
10. sultan, country: head of government
11. Beijing, capital: country
12. East China Sea, river: mouth
13. Indian Ocean, gulf: location
14. desert, place name: geographic description
15. Beirut, capital: country

Page 70
1. Israel, capital: country
2. Philippine Sea, island: location
3. China, river: location
4. Kazakhstan, geographic location
5. Taipei, capital: country
6. Japan, country: sea to the west
7. Arabian Sea, river: mouth

8. Philippine Sea, geographic location
9. wild, animal: group
10. Thailand, capital: country
11. Vietnam, geographic location
12. Sumatra/Borneo, animal: habitat (island)
13. Cambodia, capital: country
14. mountain range, place name: geographic description
15. Amman, capital: country

Page 71
1. Nepal, no coastline
2. Cambodia, not an island
3. Bombay, not a capital city
4. Gobi, not a river
5. Saudi Arabia, does not border the Mediterranean Sea
6. llama, not an Asian animal
7. Aden, not a sea
8. India, not an Arab country
9. South Korea, peninsula, only country with a coastline
10. Caspian, not a mountain range

Page 72
1. Iraq
2. Nepal/Bhutan
3. Arabian Sea/Gulf of Oman
4. Saudi Arabia
5. Myanmar
6. South China Sea
7. Sea of Japan
8. Jordan
9. Bay of Bengal
10. Afghanistan
11. Mekong River
12. Myanmar
13. East China Sea
14. Pakistan
15. Armenia

Page 73
1. Thailand
2. Mongolia
3. Saudi Arabia
4. Pakistan
5. Bangladesh
6. China
7. South Korea
8. Iran
9. Israel
10. Vietnam
11. India
12. Japan
13. Jordan
14. Turkey
15. Syria

Page 74
1. Iran
2. China
3. Saudi Arabia
4. Oman/Saudi Arabia
5. Myanmar
6. Kasakhstan
7. Jordan/Syria
8. Japan
9. India
10. Iraq
11. Pakistan
12. Vietnam
13. China
14. Turkey
15. China
16. Iraq
17. Thailand
18. China
19. Saudi Arabia/Kuwait
20. Uzbekistan

Page 75 Answers will vary.